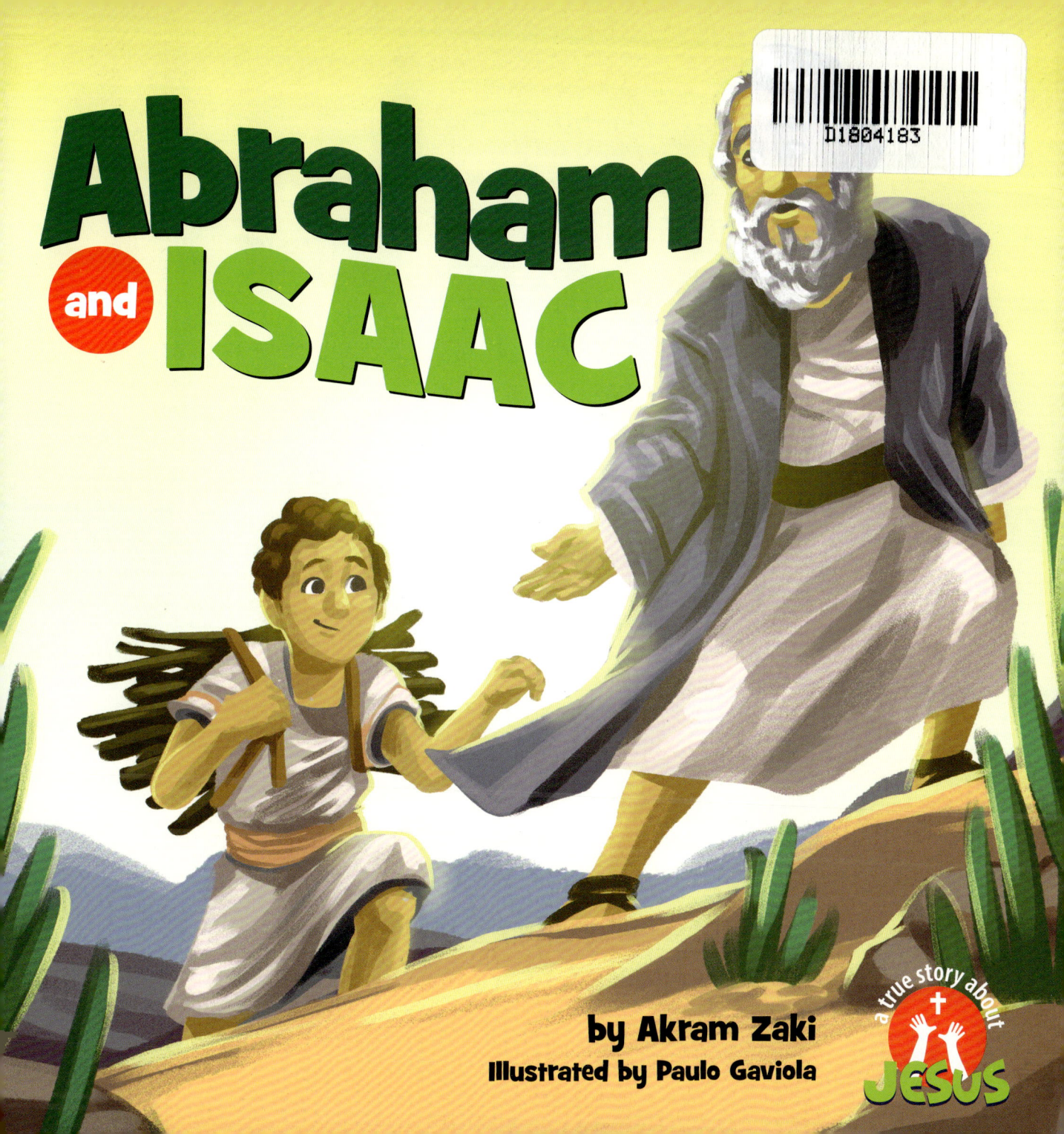

First Printing: August 2023

Copyright © 2023 by Akram Zaki. All rights reserved. No part of this book may be reproduced, copied, broadcast, stored, or shared in any form whatsoever without written permission from the publisher, except in the case of brief quotations in articles and reviews. For more information write: Master Books, PO Box 726, Green Forest, AR 72638

Master Books® is a division of the New Leaf Publishing Group, LLC.

Please consider requesting that a copy of this volume be purchased by your local library system.

ISBN: 978-1-68344-336-0
ISBN: 978-1-61458-837-5 (digital)
Library of Congress: 2023930811

Printed in China

Scripture quotations marked (NIV) are taken from the Holy Bible, New International Version®, NIV®. Copyright © 1973, 1978, 1984, 2011 by Biblica, Inc.™ Used by permission of Zondervan. All rights reserved worldwide.

Please visit our website for other great titles:
www.masterbooks.com

For information regarding promotional opportunities, please contact the publicity department at pr@nlpg.com.

This is a true story.

It comes from Genesis Chapter 22 in your Bible.

This story has some hidden things to look out for.

See if you can find them:

Long ago in Bible times, people used to make sacrifices to God. God had taught them that disobeying Him (sin) deserved death. But God loved them and gave them a way out. Instead of them dying, God told them to sacrifice a lamb.

When people saw that the lamb had died, it reminded them that God was serious about sin but that He had provided a way for them to escape, because in a way, the lamb had died in their place.

This story happened back then.

God had promised Abraham that He would give him a son. Abraham had waited many, many years, but in the end God had kept His promise when Isaac was born.

One night God spoke to Abraham.

"Abraham. Take your son, your beloved son, to a high mountain I will show you. On that mountain, I want you to sacrifice him to me as a burnt offering."

Abraham loved Isaac. But Abraham knew that God was good, that He knew what He was doing, and that He needed to be obeyed.

The next morning, Abraham took a donkey, loaded it up with wood for the sacrifice, flints to make fire, and then took His son Isaac with him.

"We have the wood and the fire for the offering," said Isaac, "But where is the lamb for the sacrifice?"

"God will provide the lamb, my son," Abraham replied.

Abraham and Isaac walked for three days until they got to a high mountain.

They left the donkey at the bottom of the mountain, and Isaac carried the wood up the mountain.

There they built an altar out of rocks and put the wood on top of it.

Abraham placed Isaac on the altar.

Abraham took out his knife, but the angel of God called to him.

"Abraham, stop! Do not lay a hand on your son. Now I know that you fear and love me. For you have not held back your beloved son from me."

Abraham looked up, and in a bush nearby was a ram (a male sheep) caught by its horns. He went over and took the ram and sacrificed it as a burnt offering instead of his son.

God accepted the sacrifice and forgave Abraham and his family for their sins. God was pleased with Abraham because he had trusted Him.

Did you find the hidden pictures?
They can help to summarize our story.

A beloved son

A high mountain

A sacrifice that God provides

Is this a story that teaches us to avoid going mountain climbing with our dads?
NO.

Is this a story that tells us that sheep get stuck in bushes a lot?
NO.

So what's this story really about?

This story is about JESUS!

But how?

The Bible tells us that sacrificing lambs and sheep could never really pay for the wrong things we have done, but those lambs are just a reminder of God's promise to rescue us from sin.

The Bible says that God has a beloved son, Jesus.

Jesus came to Earth, was born as a human, and grew up into a man.

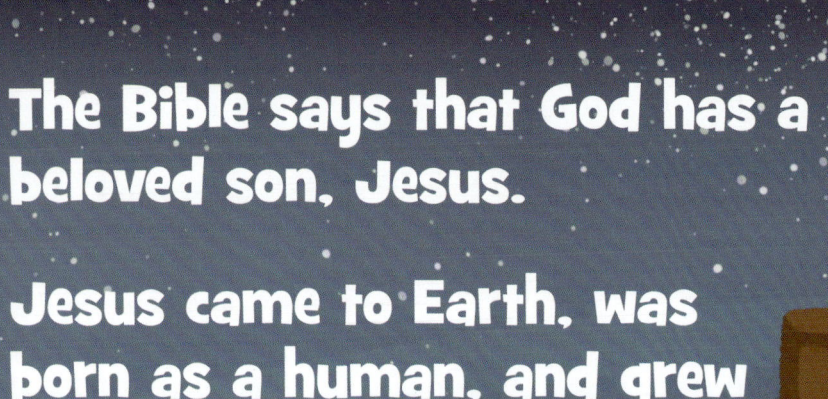

Jesus lived a perfect life, always doing what was right, and never what was wrong.

Jesus, God's beloved Son climbed a high mountain. It was called Calvary. He did it carrying wood on His back too, a wooden cross.

God knew that we could never pay for our own sin, so He provided the sacrifice needed by sending Jesus to die in our place.

Jesus was the sacrifice that God provided.

Jesus dying on the Cross shows us how serious God is about sin, but also, how much He loves us. God has provided a way for us to be rescued because Jesus has died in our place.

Jesus came back from the dead, proving that He had paid for our sin, and because of this, we can trust Him to rescue us!

For God so loved the world that he gave his one and only Son, that whoever believes in him shall not perish but have eternal life.
John 3:16 (NIV)

The next time you hear the wonderful true story about Abraham and Isaac, remember... it's a story that tells us about Jesus!